The Nature Kid's Guide to
ANACONDAS

DAVID ANDERSON

LP Media Inc. Publishing
Text copyright © 2026 by LP Media Inc.
All rights reserved.

For information address LP Media Inc. Publishing,
30012 Variolite St NW, Princeton MN 55371
www.lpmedia.org

Publication Data

Anacondas
The Nature Kid's Guide to Anacondas — First edition.

Summary: "Learn all about Anacondas, the Nature Kid Way"
— Provided by publisher.

ISBN: 979-8-89818-229-8

[1. Anacondas – Non-Fiction] I. Title.

Title: The Nature Kid's Guide to Anacondas

CONTENTS

SWAMPY SPOTS

A green anaconda can hold its breath and stay under water for up to ten minutes!

Splash! A green anaconda slides into a warm, murky swamp.

Green anacondas love wet, warm places. They live in swamps, marshes, and slow rivers where thick plants grow all around them.

The water helps hold up their big, heavy bodies. These snakes hide under the surface with just their eyes poking out. This helps them stay cool and watch for prey at the same time.

These snakes call the rain forest home. They need warm air and lots of water to survive. A swamp is the perfect spot for them.

SOUTH AMERICA
FUN FACT!
Some anacondas live on the island of Trinidad, swimming between flooded forests!
6

Hiss! A yellow anaconda peeks out from the wet grass.

Anacondas live in South America. You can find them in Brazil, Peru, Colombia, and Bolivia. They do not live in cold places.

Yellow anacondas live farther to the south in the wetlands of Paraguay and Argentina. The weather there is a bit cooler, but still warm enough for these snakes.

Most anacondas stay near rivers and lakes. They need warm, wet land all year long. You will not spot them in deserts or mountains.

SUPER SIZED

Thump! A huge, heavy anaconda drags its body across the mud.

Green anacondas are the heaviest snakes on Earth. A big one can weigh over 200 pounds. That is more than most grown-ups!

They can grow longer than a car. Some reach over 20 feet long, and their body can be as thick as a dinner plate. Picture a snake stretched across your whole classroom!

These are truly giant reptiles. No other snake on Earth weighs as much as a green anaconda.

Green anacondas never stop growing — they get bigger every single year of their lives!

BUILT STRONG

Crunch! Strong muscles help an anaconda coil around a branch.

Anacondas have strong, stretchy bodies covered in smooth, dry scales. Their scales are dark green with black spots that help them hide.

Since they have no arms or legs, anacondas use hundreds of ribs and powerful muscles to move. Their jaw can open super wide to swallow meals bigger than their own head!

Small eyes sit on top of their head. This lets them see above the water while the rest of their body stays hidden below. Every part of an anaconda is built for life in the swamp.

TONGUE TASTE

Anacondas do not have outer ears, but they feel sounds through their jaw bones!

Flick! An anaconda darts its tongue out to taste the air.

Anacondas use their tongue to smell. They flick it out fast to pick up tiny bits from the air. Then the tongue brings them back to a special spot in their mouth that reads the smells.

Their eyes are not very sharp. But anacondas can feel vibrations in the ground and water. This tells them when animals are moving nearby.

Anacondas also have small pits near their lips. These pits sense heat from other animals. It is like having a built-in heat finder that works even in total darkness.

HIDE WELL

When threatened, an anaconda can release a smell so stinky that predators run away!

DID YOU KNOW?

Shhh! A green anaconda hides among the floating leaves.

Anacondas have great **camouflage**. Their dark green and brown colors help them blend in with murky water and plants. They look just like part of the swamp.

When danger comes, they slip into water. Under the surface, they are nearly impossible to spot. They can stay perfectly still for hours.

Their huge size keeps them safe too. Most animals will not mess with such a giant snake. Being big is one of the best defenses in the wild.

BIG BITES

Anacondas sometimes eat capybaras — rodents that weigh up to 140 pounds!

Gulp! An anaconda swallows a whole bird in one big bite.

Anacondas eat many kinds of animals. They catch fish, birds, and turtles. They also hunt larger prey like deer and wild pigs.

Big anacondas can even eat caimans. A caiman is like a small alligator with sharp teeth. It takes a very strong snake to catch one of those!

After a huge meal, an anaconda may not eat for weeks or even months. Its body needs time to break down all that food. One big meal can keep them going for a long time.

SQUEEZE TIGHT

An anaconda squeezes tighter each time its prey breathes out — there is no escape!

18

Snap! An anaconda grabs its prey and wraps around tight.

Anacondas are **ambush** hunters. They wait very still in the water, sometimes for hours. When an animal comes close, they strike in a flash.

First, they grab with their sharp teeth. Then they wrap their strong body around the prey and squeeze. They squeeze until the animal can no longer breathe.

Anacondas do not use venom or poison. They use only their powerful muscles. This way of hunting is called **constriction**, and anacondas are masters at it.

WATCH OUT

DID YOU KNOW?
Giant otters sometimes gang up in groups of six or more to chase anacondas away!

Roar! A big jaguar spots a resting anaconda by the river.

Even big anacondas have enemies. Jaguars are one of the few animals brave enough to fight them. Large **caimans** may attack too.

Young anacondas face much more danger. Hawks, foxes, and big fish may eat them. Small snakes have a harder time staying safe in the wild.

As anacondas grow, they have fewer predators. Their huge size scares most animals away. Very few creatures dare to challenge a full-grown anaconda.

SLIP AWAY

FUN FACT!
An anaconda can swim about 10 miles per hour — that's as fast as you can run!

Swoosh! A scared anaconda dives under the water to escape.

Water is the best escape plan for an anaconda. They slide under and swim away fast. In water, they move much better than on land.

When an anaconda feels danger, it does not always fight. Slipping away quietly is often the smarter choice. Most times, they just want to be left alone.

If caught, an anaconda may bite hard. Its many backward-curving teeth help it break free. Then it dashes to the nearest water as fast as it can.

DID YOU KNOW?

Young anacondas sometimes climb into small trees to rest, hunt, or escape danger!

24

Swish! A yellow anaconda glides through the shallow water.

Anacondas are great swimmers. They push their body in S-shaped curves through the water. Their muscles ripple smoothly from head to tail.

On land, they are much slower and clumsier. Moving on the ground is hard work for such a heavy snake. They slide along using their belly scales to grip the dirt.

Yellow anacondas are a bit smaller than green ones, but they still move the same way. Both kinds swim far better than they crawl.

LAZY DAYS

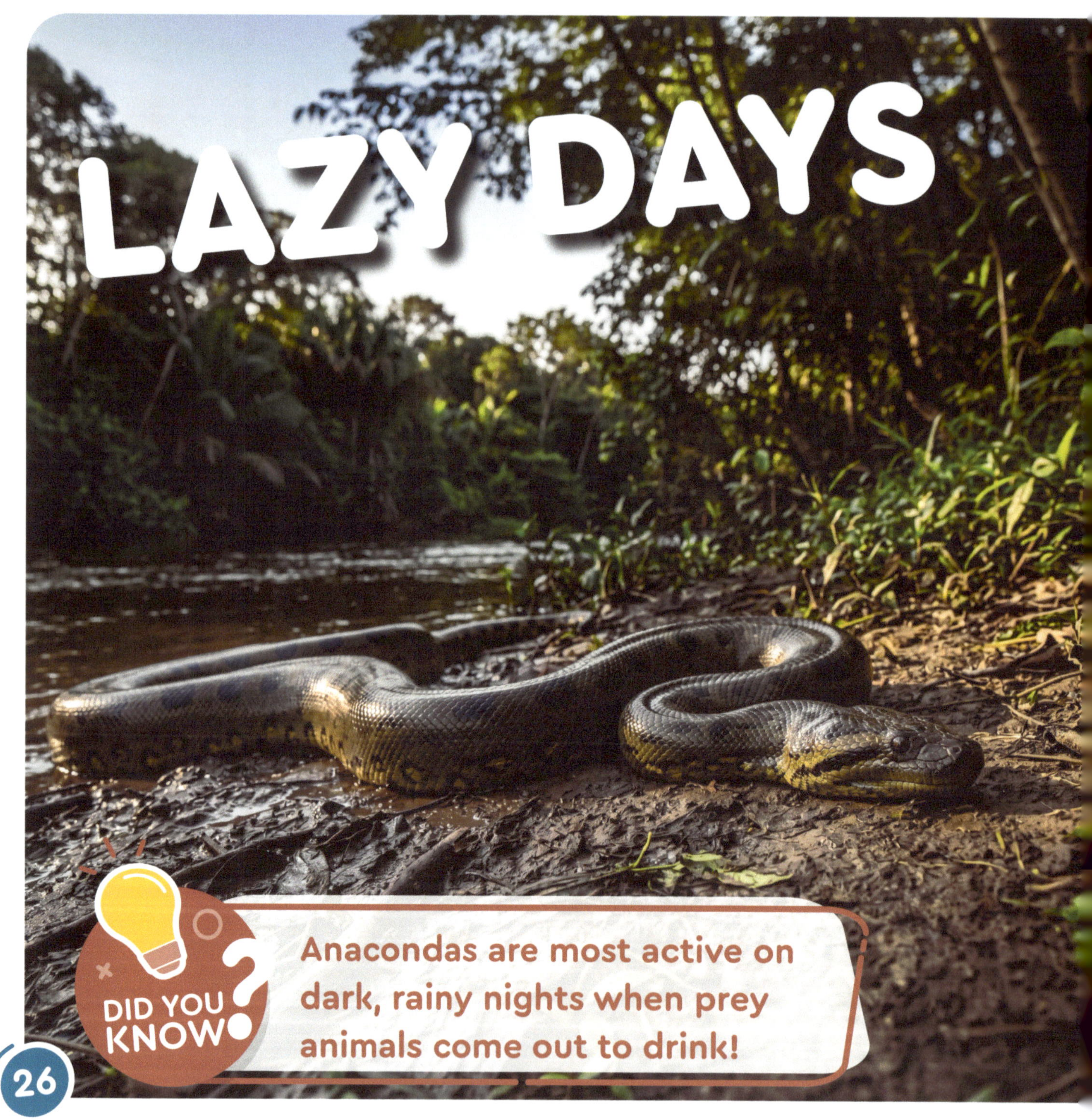

DID YOU KNOW?
Anacondas are most active on dark, rainy nights when prey animals come out to drink!

Zzzz! A big anaconda soaks in the morning sun by the river.

Anacondas spend a lot of time resting. They lie in shallow water or on a muddy bank. Warm sun helps their **cold-blooded** bodies stay healthy and strong.

These snakes are more active at night. They hunt in the dark when the air is cool. Their heat-sensing pits work well even without any light.

After a big meal, they barely move for days or weeks. They rest while their body slowly breaks down the food. Being still helps them save energy for the next hunt.

SOLO SNAKES

FUN FACT!

28

Rustle! A lone anaconda slides through thick grass alone.

Anacondas are solitary animals. They live and hunt alone most of the time. You will rarely see two together.

Each anaconda has its own home area. It knows the best spots to hunt and the safest places to rest. They do not share space with other snakes.

The only time anacondas come together is to mate. After that, they go right back to being alone. These snakes truly enjoy their own company.

MATING BALLS

Up to twelve male anacondas may pile into one single breeding ball!

Slap! A ball of snakes rolls and twists by the water.

At mating time, many males look for one female. They all wrap around her in a tangled group called a breeding ball. It looks like a giant knot of snakes!

The males push and shove to be closest to her. This wrestling match can go on for two to four weeks! The strongest male usually wins.

Female anacondas are much bigger than males. A mother can be two or three times heavier than the males around her. She is always the biggest snake in the group.

WIGGLY BABIES

Slither! A newborn anaconda slithers on the forest floor.

Anacondas do not lay eggs like many snakes do. The babies grow inside their mother instead. When ready, she gives birth to live young.

A mother can have 20 to 40 babies at once! Each baby is about two feet long and looks like a tiny copy of mom. Some mothers have even more babies than that.

The babies can swim and hunt right away. They do not need any help from their parents. From day one, they are ready to survive on their own.

GO SOLO

DID YOU KNOW?
Only about half of baby anacondas survive their dangerous first year of life!

34

Poof! The mother slips away and the babies are on their own.

Mother anacondas do not stay with their babies. After birth, the mother leaves right away. The tiny snakes must care for themselves from the very first moment.

Baby anacondas must find food and stay safe all alone. They learn fast or they may not survive. Life starts out tough for these little snakes.

At first, babies eat small things like frogs, little fish, and lizards. As they grow bigger, they hunt bigger prey. Each year, their meals get larger too.

ANCIENT SNAKES
DID YOU KNOW?
The Titanoboa grew up to 42 feet long and weighed over 2,500 pounds!
36

Ssss! Anacondas have slithered on Earth for millions of years.

Anacondas belong to one of the oldest snake families on Earth, called the boas. This family has been around for over 60 million years, long before most other snake families even existed.

The boa family is huge. Boa constrictors, emerald tree boas, rainbow boas, and rubber boas are all cousins of the anaconda. They live on five continents and come in dozens of shapes and sizes.

But the most jaw-dropping relative of all was the Titanboa. They lived millions of years ago and make even the green anaconda look small.

SPOT ONE!
FUN FACT!
Some zoos keep anacondas in pools large enough to swim full laps — the water has to be kept warm all year round to keep them healthy!
38

Splash! An anaconda glides slowly along the edge of its zoo enclosure.

You do not have to travel to South America to see an anaconda up close. Many zoos across the United States keep green anacondas, and some reptile parks and nature centers have them too.

When you visit, watch how they move, how they breathe, and how incredibly thick their bodies really are. Ask a keeper when feeding time is — watching an anaconda eat is something you will never forget.

If you ever do visit South America, trained wildlife guides can take you to safe spots along rivers where wild anacondas rest and swim.

GLOSSARY

ambush
To hide and wait, then attack by surprise

camouflage
Colors or patterns that help an animal blend in and hide

caiman
A reptile like a small alligator that lives in South America

constriction
Killing prey by squeezing it very tightly

cold-blooded
An animal that cannot make its own body heat and relies on outside warmth to stay active